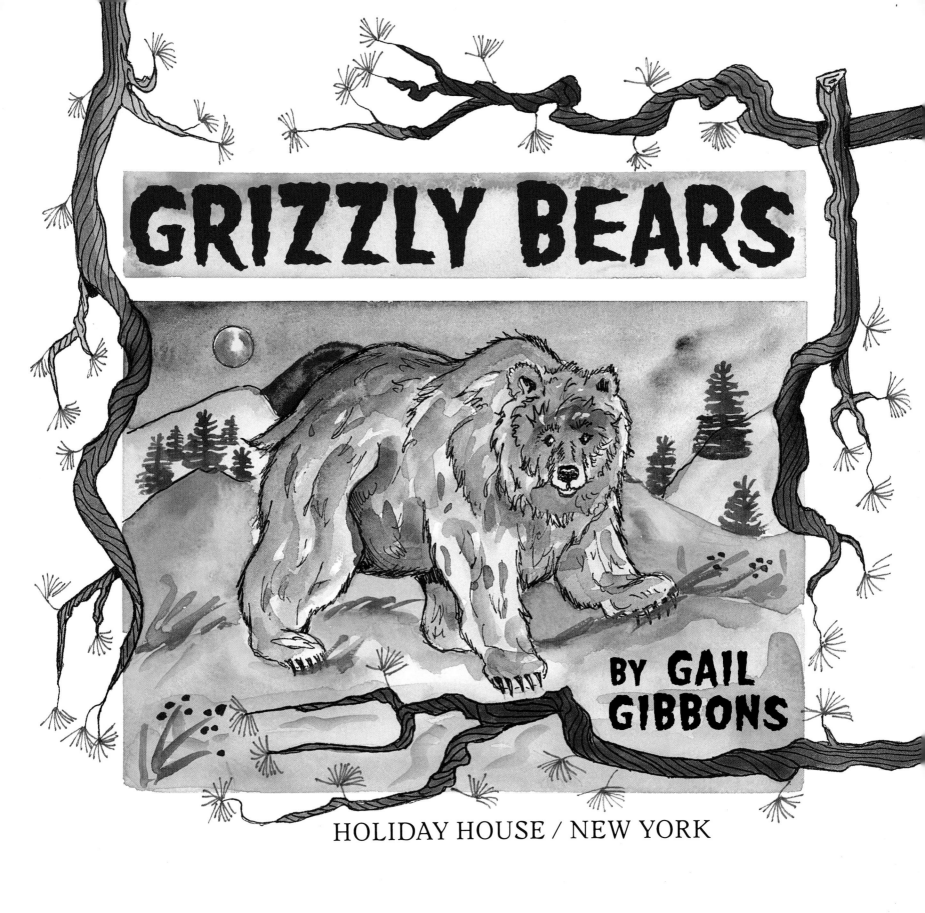

GRIZZLY BEARS

BY GAIL GIBBONS

HOLIDAY HOUSE / NEW YORK

To the children
at the Sprague School,
Lincolnshire, Illinois

Special thanks
to James Doherty,
general curator
at the New York Zoological Society,
Bronx, New York

Library of Congress Cataloging-in-Publication Data
Gibbons, Gail.
Grizzly bears / by Gail Gibbons.—1st ed.
p.   cm
Summary: Introduces the physical characteristics, behavior, and life cycle of grizzly
bears, and discusses their endangerment in the lower forty-eight United States.
ISBN 0-8234-1793-X (hardcover)
1. Grizzly bear—Juvenile literature. [1. Grizzly bear. 2. Bears.
3. Endangered species.] I. Title.

QL737.C27G4797 2003
599.784—dc21
2003049992

ISBN-13: 978-0-8234-1793-3

SALMON swim upstream to find places to lay their eggs.

GRIZZLY BEAR

It is early summer in the northwestern region of North America. A large bear spots salmon swimming upstream against the rushing water. With one powerful motion, the animal lunges forward into the stream. It grabs a salmon for food as the fish leaps by. The bear is a grizzly bear.

The scientific name for GRIZZLY BEAR is URSUS ARCTOS HORRIBILIS, meaning "horrible bear."

Many scientists believe the bear family, called Ursus, evolved from the dog family about 20 million years ago. Around 3 million years ago they began to look like the bears we know today. The grizzly bear is a member of the brown bear family.

WHERE GRIZZLY BEARS
ONCE LIVED

WHERE GRIZZLY BEARS
LIVE TODAY

ALASKA

CANADA

UNITED STATES

MEXICO

At one time grizzly bears lived in most of North America. As settlers moved west, many grizzlies were killed for food and for their fur. Sometimes hungry bears attacked livestock and were killed by settlers. Today grizzlies live in a small part of the United States.

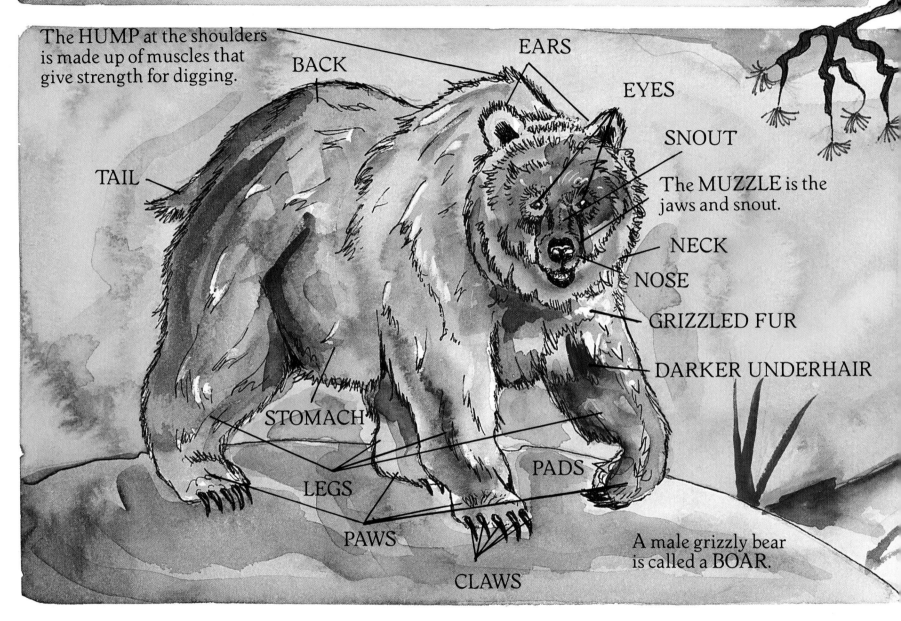

The HUMP at the shoulders is made up of muscles that give strength for digging.

BACK

EARS

EYES

SNOUT

The MUZZLE is the jaws and snout.

TAIL

NECK

NOSE

GRIZZLED FUR

DARKER UNDERHAIR

STOMACH

PADS

LEGS

PAWS

A male grizzly bear is called a BOAR.

CLAWS

Grizzly bears get their name from the silvery white tips of their fur. These silvery tips make their fur look "grizzled," or as if the bears were going gray. Some grizzlies are tan colored; others are reddish. Some are brown or almost black. All grizzlies have a prominent shoulder hump, a short muzzle that gives their faces a flattened look, and thick, straight claws.

A female grizzly bear is called a SOW.

An adult grizzly bear is usually 6 to 8 feet (1.8 to 2.4 m) long. Most adult males weigh 400 to 600 pounds (180 to 230 kg). Most adult females weigh between 350 and 400 pounds (160 and 180 kg). A grizzly's thick, coarse fur keeps its body dry and warm.

A grizzly bear can HEAR better than a person.

A grizzly bear can SMELL a dead animal miles away.

Grizzly bears have poor eyesight. But they make up for that by using their excellent sense of smell. They use their sense of smell to search for food and to alert them to danger. Grizzlies have a good sense of hearing, too.

When a grizzly bear moves about in the wild, it appears to be a slow-moving animal. But when it wants to, its can run 35 to 45 miles (56.3 to 72.4 km) an hour. That is as fast as a horse can run.

CUB

Grizzlies are good swimmers. Cubs are able to climb tall trees.

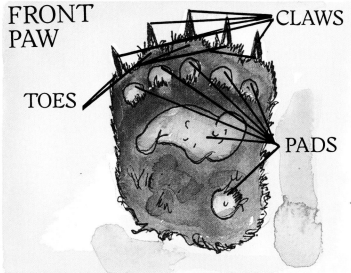

FRONT PAW

CLAWS

TOES

PADS

When grizzly bears stand on their hind legs, they are from 8 to 10 feet (2.4 to 3 m) tall.

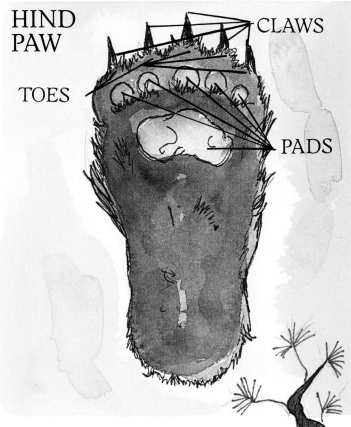

HIND PAW

CLAWS

TOES

PADS

Grizzly bears have short legs and flat hind paws that help them to stand. Each paw has five toes with claws that are about 4 inches (10.6 cm) long. The claws on their front paws are used for digging and protection.

Grizzlies live independent lives. Some live their entire lives within a few square miles. Others roam great distances.

A TUBER is a fleshy underground stem.

Grizzly bears will eat almost anything. They eat a lot of berries, nuts, honey, grasses, roots, and tubers. They use their straight claws for digging foods they want to eat from under the ground.

Their MOLARS are used for grinding food.

Their CANINE TEETH can be 2 inches (5 cm) long. They are used for gripping and tearing food.

Grizzlies are OMNIVORES. That means they eat plants and animals.

Grizzly bears also eat meat. Grizzlies have pointed canine teeth to help them catch and kill small and large animals as well as fish.

During the spring, grizzly bears eat 25 to 35 pounds (11.3 to 15.8 kg) of food a day. In the fall they eat 100 pounds (45.3 kg) of food a day to put on weight for the long winter months to come. Some of the biggest grizzlies live along salmon-filled streams. The salmon they catch are nutritious.

Male grizzlies make their dens, too.

In the early part of the summer, the male and female grizzly bears mate. By the time winter sets in, a female grizzly has stored up enough fat in her body to survive the winter without food. It is time to prepare her den.

Some dens are
inside CAVES.

DEN

The female uses her strong forearms and sharp claws to dig her den in a hillside. The den is slightly higher than its entrance to keep the inside dry throughout the coming winter months. It is time for her to hibernate.

Snow seals the entrance from cold north winds.

Hibernation means she will sleep and rest throughout the winter. She now has 6 to 10 inches (15.2 to 25.4 cm) of fat under her skin to keep her warm and provide nutrition. Her body temperature drops just a few degrees, but her heart rate slows down from forty beats a minute to about ten beats a minute.

A mother grizzly bear can give birth to one to four cubs.

CUB

In the early part of the year, the female grizzly begins moving about. She gives birth to two tiny cubs. Their mother immediately begins nursing them as she gently holds them. The cubs are tiny. They weigh about 1 pound (.45 kg) each.

The newborn cubs' eyes are closed. They are helpless. Their small bodies are covered with a coat of very fine fur. Their mother continues nursing them with her milk, which is rich in fat.

By early springtime, the cubs are about 3 months old and weigh about 5 pounds (2.2 kg). The cubs don't leave their den until they have grown thick coats of fur. Now their eyes are open, and they are able to walk. Their mother gently nudges them out of the den.

The cubs stay close to their mother. Immediately, she begins looking for food. The cubs learn by watching their mother and eating what she eats. They learn to hunt, too. Grizzly bear cubs are full of energy. As they play, they learn the skills they will need when they grow up.

The mother grizzly is extremely protective of her cubs. Sometimes a male grizzly bear might try to attack her cubs, but their mother is a fierce fighter. Often the cubs run up a tree for safety. Most often the male leaves. The mother goes back to caring for her cubs.

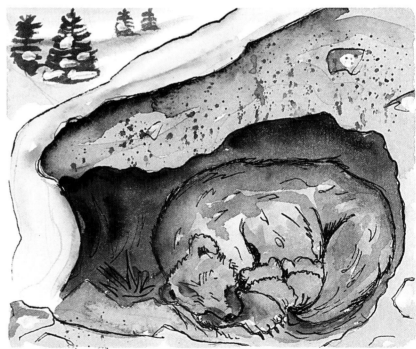

Over time the cubs grow bigger and bigger. Throughout the warmer weather they learn many things to survive in the wild. Cold wind blows. Snow comes along with winter again. The mother and her cubs hibernate in their den.

Once again springtime comes. The grizzly bear cubs are much bigger now. Their mother stops nursing them. This is called weaning. When the cubs are about 1½ to 2½ years old, the mother will chase them away, signaling that her bear cubs are ready to live on their own. When the females are about 5 years old, they will be able to raise their own young.

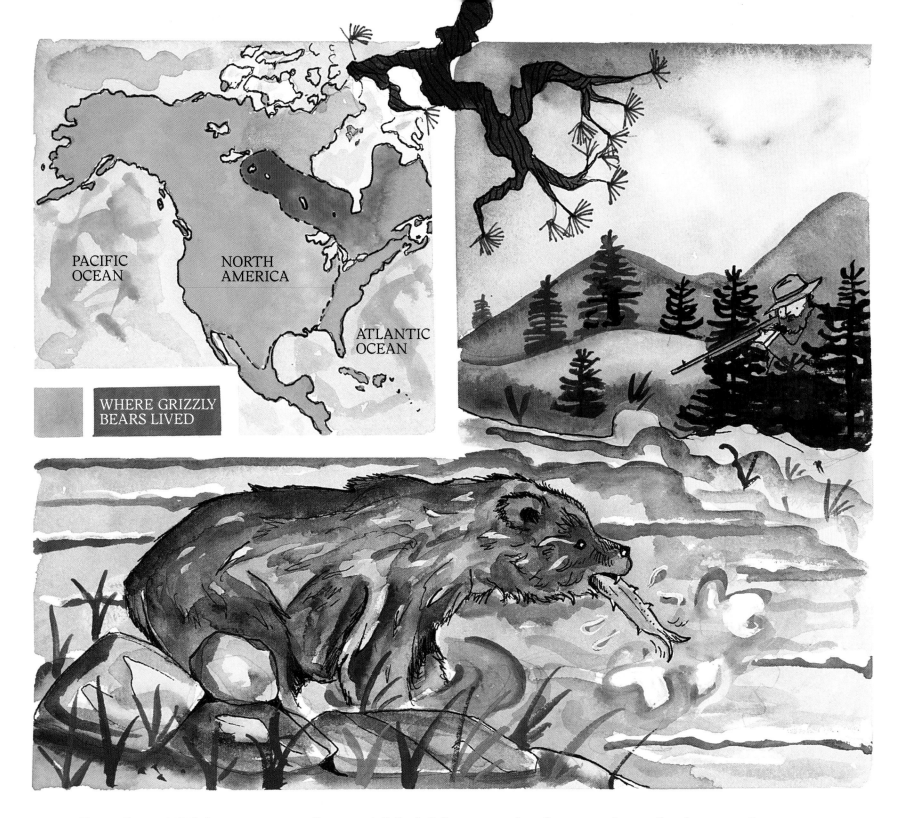

In the 1700s, more than 100,000 grizzly bears lived throughout most of North America. They roamed as far east as the Mississippi River. People became their only enemies.

GRIZZLY BEARS
LIVE HERE

WATERTON LAKES
NATIONAL PARK

CANADA

WASHINGTON

GLACIER NATIONAL
PARK

MONTANA

IDAHO

YELLOWSTONE
NATIONAL PARK

WYOMING

Today about 50,000 grizzly bears live in Alaska and Canada. Only about 800 live in Montana, Wyoming, Washington, and Idaho. The grizzly bears in the lower forty-eight states of the United States are threatened with extinction. Most of them live in national parks.

Because grizzlies in the United States are threatened with extinction, scientists try to find ways of protecting them. Sometimes radio collars are put around the bears' necks to track them. This helps scientists keep accurate records of where the grizzlies are living and how they are doing in the wild.

In 1975 the Endangered Species Act was established and included the protection of grizzly bears in the lower forty-eight states. People are warned to stay away from grizzly bears. On some occasions grizzlies have attacked people, usually when protecting their cubs or their territory.

Today most people only see grizzly bears in zoos.

Hopefully, over time the numbers of grizzly bears will increase in their natural environments. They should never vanish from the forests and woods where they belong.

GRIZZLY BEAR FOOTPRINTS...

Most grizzlies live to be 20 to 30 years old.

The largest grizzly bear ever recorded weighed 1,400 pounds (635 kg).

One grizzly bear at the Omaha Zoo in Nebraska lived to be 40 years old.

About 90 percent of a grizzly's diet is made up of plant life.

Grizzlies can put on 100 pounds (45.3 kg) of extra fat to get through the winter.

When camping where there might be bears, keep all foods away from your campsite.

A grizzly bear can eat 200,000 berries in one day!

NEVER try to feed a grizzly bear in the wild.

Many grizzlies may come together when they are catching salmon.

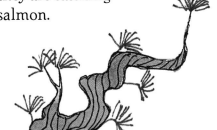

NEVER run away from a grizzly bear. If one threatens to charge you, lay on the ground, roll up in a ball, and lay perfectly still. That way the bear will know you are not aggressive.